Sister in a Different Movie

Sister in a Different Movie

poems

Laura Foley

Sheila-Na-Gig Editions

Acknowledgments

Grateful acknowledgment is made to the editors of the journals and anthologies who first published the following poems. The poems, sometimes in earlier versions, appeared as follows:

Autumn Sky: "Mermaids," "Small Certainties"
Black Coffee Review: "Special Delivery"
Eclectica Magazine: "The Good Kind of Chill"
Gyroscope Review: "Cloud Gazing"
Little Free Lit Magazine: "Dodes'ka-den"
MacQueen's Quinterly: "The Mosquitoes of Tatamagouche"
Midwest Quarterly: "Now the Repairman," "The River House"
One Art: "Coming Out to My Sister," "Dust of Snow," "Let's
    Go Out for Breakfast. . .," "Tea and Sympathy"
One Jacar Press: "Jumble"
Pensive Journal: "Watching the News From Afghanistan"
Poetry Breakfast: "After a Migraine"
Red-Headed Stepchild: "As Shadows Lengthen"
Rock Paper Poem: "Sketching"
Schuylkill Valley Journal: "Poem to My Fallopian Tube"
Sheila-Na-Gig online: "The Steward"
Silver Birch Press: "Mom's Dreams"
Sunlight Press: "Little Darts"
Valparaiso Poetry Review: "Sister in the Old Country"

Prizes

Blue Mesa Review Poetry Prize: "The Summer-Lessened Stream"
Hungry Hill Writing: Poets Meet Politics Poetry Competition:
    "Beneath the Snow"
Narrative Magazine Poetry Contest: "Amaryllis"
Naugatuck River Review Poetry Prize: "A Gated Community"

For my sister Claire, in memory

Contents

*A sister is like yourself in a different movie,
a movie that stars you in a different life.*

—Deborah Tannen

♀

On the Verge

Trees freed from autumn's
arias of color,
the loud ground
quieted of crickets and toads.

A subtler time
when every hour of sun
is a quaff
against the growing night.

How urgent
every ray of light
when we wake
on the verge
of lifelessness.

Small Certainties

I was lucky—
born fourth
of four girls, so Dad
had a little more time
to get over the war—

even so, at the dining table,
glittering with candles,
platters of roast beef,
potatoes, green beans—
always the talk of starvation,
water torture.

He had endured
four winters in prison in China,
worked in a salt mine.

I felt proud of him,
though terribly shy,
and would slip away
to my room.

Still, I was lucky—
I didn't see the worms
one sister imagined
wriggling in the rugs,

didn't leap from a window
onto barbed wire,
as another sister did,

but learned instead
to seek joy
in the smallest ways,
lining up my toy cats—

small, bright certainties
in a world still trembling
from what came before.

The River House

with its western-facing
ocean of afternoon sun,
its view of shifting surfaces.

Widowed, then wedded
to emptiness, to the iron
steps reaching down
to water's edge,
craggy mountain rising up,
with dust of snow,
or shadowed moon—

how I would pace from room
to cavernous Victorian room,
narrow, uneven stairs,
as wind rattled the walls,
trying to let the unknown in.

How an eagle seized
a salmon, yellow talons
ripping pink flesh open.

How warped wooden floors
creaked, tilting riverward,
how icy snow careened
from the steep roof,
in a tumult of longing.

Sister in the Old Country

Wicklow Road, County Cavan. Sixteen,
I visit nanny Mrs. D.'s sister, who at seventy-five
still rides a bike, wears a pink flowered dress
I recognize as a hand-me-down from Mom. We sit
in the kitchen, a circle of women on metal chairs,
Christ smiling from the wall despite his bleeding heart.
She says the rosary and we repeat, *Blessed is the fruit,*
full of grace, thy womb. . . Crones' voices droning,
like ancient druids, echoing in the linoleum-tiled room.
Aromas of puddings, soda bread baking, mouth-watering
odor of onions, eggs, mutton, tomatoes fried in fat.
Faces like pale stones, hardened, weather-worn.
Outside, the acrid smell of burning peat, damp earth
and salt air—the sacred, encircling sea.

Sketching

I'm not spending the rest of my life
trying to sketch him back in,
but sometimes he insists—
appearing behind me in the mirror,
combing over his balding dome,
thin gray wisps the wind lifts
like the wings of his *Chauve Souris*
sailing in the Tall Ships armada,
then through the Panama Canal
down to the Galapagos.

Mostly he sleeps in darkness
and silence, like bats in my attic,
but I glimpse him fleeting
in our children's faces,
or memories rise like mist
from a river of us—
our travels with our three young ones
in Machu Picchu, in Peruvian jungles,
in a long river canoe,
a guide shining his light
into a caiman's orange eyes—
though now I hold our grandchild on my lap,
sun setting on a snowy mid-winter day,
well into another century,
me married again—

when I least expect it,
he flies right past me,
as I bend over a desk, sketching.

In Living Color

My wife hangs a cascade of colors
on the staircase wall—
our yellow Lab leaping in snow,
red kayak misted in lake-fog,
me walking a snowy beach,
us kissing
beneath rainbow flags in Spain.
I hear her steps
up and down the wooden stairs,
then up and down again,
as she tends to our memories,
violet Easter eggs
next to us cradling granddaughters,
her bow tie
matching my orange jacket,
a whale breaching sea waves.
I hear her steps up and down
the wooden stairs
while I wash a white page
with her Spanish accent's
spicy lavender,
as she answers the phone
in our sun-lit, gray house,
its red doors on a hill,
a sticky, hot summer day,
bathed by a purple wave—
two dogs snoring at my feet.

Prism

When a summer wind tips
a vase of flowers into the sink
and Dad finds the splinters,
he bellows at Mom—pregnant with me—

his nerves still raw
from four years as prisoner of war,
his wounds still glistening,
red as raspberries.

Those shards stay with me,
bright fragments I see
each time my sister Claire
slams her hand in a car door, sniffs glue,

watches snakes and panthers
slide through the edges of her mind—
shards that cut her,
no matter how carefully she walks.

I hold mine to the light—the shard
of brokenness I use to cast brightness
back across the past, seeking what gleams
in memory's darker rooms,

like daffodils nodding in a clear glass jar
from Mom's cupboard—
her grace a small sun
at the center of our table.

The Softening

Recently widowed,
the window's swirling flakes
a shaken snow globe,
I stood in my kitchen
with hungry children
commotioning for dinner,

phone cradled to my ear
as I cooked, my sister Claire's lawyer
ranted about her badgering,
her imagining a million-dollar theft—

his voice suddenly softening
like butter in the sun:
I feel sorry for you,
having a sibling like this.
Toddler astride my hip,

I salted the pasta with my free hand,
as his soft pity weakened my knees,
made it harder for me
to stir and strain and serve—

as the snow globe filled,
and something in me
dissolved
like salt in a wound.

Mom's Dreams

The worst, she said,
were when she had to choose

one out of four daughters,
watch the other children drown.

She said this lightly, as the two of us
picnicked in a maple's waving shadows,

on grass fresh and clean as a new beginning,
as we drove cross country that summer.

She let me choose motels—
the teddy bear my favorite.

She sometimes let me steer,
throw quarters in the toll basket,

or nap, my head heavy on her soft lap
as she smoked, filling the ashtray

with lipsticked filters, while I savored
the familiar acrid scent.

I don't know if either of us sensed
she did save me from the drowning depths

of Dad's rage, older sisters' mayhem—
or what we might have done differently,

if we had known her love
could save only one of us.

Held

Try sitting by a pond,
as neon-blue dragonflies
alight on your knee,

one, then two,
then they slowly intertwine,
trusting your body as they would
reed or stone or branch.

Strip off sun hat, shoes, socks, shirt—
slip deep into the rain-filled pond,
cooling hot skin.

Let your body float,
surrounded by sky-tall reeds,
as you watch, and are watched by,
the infinite cloudlessness above.

Know you're in the eye of it,
held by, and holding, summer.

The Cut Field

—with a line by Elizabeth Bishop

the owner died
a week ago
the field it seems
has mowed itself

some friend or ghost
or roving god—
back and forth
back and forth
revise revise revise
to get it right

no farmer now
to steer
the old John Deere

only hay
drying in heat

another season
just begun

June's bright blooms
bone-bleached
seeds scattered
like ashes in sun.

The Thief

After my oldest sister's surgery,
her voice raspy on the phone—

so faint I can't hear.

By email she explains—

"Someone breached security,
broke into my room,

stole my voice…

Very little pain," she assures.

       They've replaced her knee,

but they can't revive
her stolen, spark-less mind

or find the thief.

Dust of Snow

I thought I was done
mourning war,
learning again to savor

a faceful of snow
shaken from the pine—
a small blessing—

without remembering
water dripping on my father's head,
the torture, the coma,

his four years
in a Japanese prison
before he became my father.

And Stefan, too—
skiing out of Poland,
escape carved through snow

into Lithuania, then Russia,
before he became my husband—
now gone these many years.

This dawn after snowfall,
as a new war enters my thoughts,
sun lifts a thin white line

from the chimney
of our gray, peaceable house
on its wooded hill.

Still, I see smoke
from bombed buildings,
barely noticing

how snow loosens
from the pine's arms,
drifting like a quiet ghost.

Coming Out to My Sister

My sister—
the aloof one—
wasn't, that day.
She took my arm,
led me through Georgetown,
sunlight on brick sidewalks,
into a small boutique
where we found clothes
soft as permission.

I chose a black silk cape,
delicate women stitched
across the back—
a garment that felt
like stepping into myself.

For a little while
she smiled at me,
held the clothes to my shoulders,
wanting to see
who I might become.

Many years now
she hasn't called,
doesn't answer emails—
has slipped again
into distance, into silence.

But the cape still hangs
in my closet,
light as breath,
reminding me
of the one day
we were gentle
with each other.

Amaryllis

My oldest sister sends me
and our other sister
an amaryllis for Christmas
just as Dad used to. Who
wouldn't like such a gift?
Just water the boxed dirt,
and up she'll push, rising
in red-streaked blossoms,
filling a winter room with color.
But my other sister screams
from three thousand miles away,
via satellite, "It's phallic!" throws
the plant in the trash, angered
by this supposed intrusion
of his maleness, thirty years
past Dad's death,
never mind it's named
for Virgil's shepherdess.
I've just watched
a newly discovered
1983 TV interview with Dad,
finding myself pleased
to see him, now I'm almost
his age. Dapper in gray suit,
patterned bow tie,
he recounts famous patients,
Chiang Kai-shek's letter,
but I'm struck
by his shallow breathing,
tightness of chest,
the parched way
he licks his lips. Was this
man in pain we never noticed?
Did the prominent heart
doctor have a heart ailment

he tried to hide?
I've long since put away
my blaming, so when the plant
arrives half-frozen, I give it water,
await its namesake,
hope it thrives.

♀♀

A Gated Community

Claire loved the security
of the guard, and the gate

lifting for her car
keeping her safe,

until the night
she immersed

in a hot bath
and her heart seized—

she sank down,
drowned,

the water still running
from the taps, water

overflowing the tub,
seeping under the door,

soaking the rug, water
deepening for two weeks,

until it wept through
the neighbor's wall—

then came—
police breaking

the locked door of her life,
finding she'd escaped

to a place beyond water,
where she'll always feel safe—

my sister, who loved real estate,
at peace, beyond the gates.

The Steward

—for Ad Shaw 1931-2021

How a single wren still warbles on the topmost branch
of a swaying poplar tree

how dandelions still appear
like scattered suns lighting a grassy field

how the unknowing field rests unmown,
long enough to host the nesting bobolink

how the field's steward abided for many seasons of late haying,
leaf fall, ice and deep snow, knowing he couldn't stay

how a dragonfly tastes the dew from a flower,
pauses on my knee as if to speak

how my focus shifts to his old window
in the vale, just beyond the reedy pond

how wood thrush, just returned,
sing their liquid notes in the cool hemlock shade

but return to silence
when the sun emerges from a cloud

how the day still breaks
into spring's first heat

Jumble

I lack the words to evoke five o'clock
emptiness—no aromas of garlic,
no paprika, no sweetness of flan
tempting my nose, no tomatoes
fried in finest olive oil to slick my tongue,
like the Spanish syllables she needs
to hear spoken in Madrid's highlands,
where her siblings & ninety-year-old
mother have missed her. But what's the use
my searching for words?
By the time I finish this, she'll be home,
where she's meant to be, with me,
her boots a cozy jumble
by our door, spooning my shoes.

Now the Repairman

My voice across the wires pierces the repairman's ears in
Texas: *This was my sister, Ears in Texas! Blood you left a month
after her passing, Ears in Texas!* Remembering her nine years to
my four: *Look at those bloody hands* her paranoia saw pointing
to the faucet. So I wouldn't get in the bath with her? No
Macbeth, my sister's blood was her own, tub her own,
though my lawyer assures no fault in her dying flood. Her
neighbors have no right to sue an Act of God, how God or
faucets act, the running water flooding both townhouses.
God, or Claire's mischief? The repairman sends scrubbed
tub photos, so I can stop shouting through her laughter.
Now the repairman. Now the repair. My cold empty tub
holding me like the sister I've missed since childhood.

My voice   wires   the repairman's ears in Texas   *my sister
Ears   Texas   Blood you left after her passing   Texas*   Remember
her nine years   *Look at those bloody hands*   pointing to the
faucet   So I wouldn't   Macbeth my sister's blood   tub
her own   no fault in   dying   go sue an Act of God   or
faucets   flooding   townhouses   God's mischief   The
repairman sends scrubbed tub photos   shouting through
her laughter   repair   My cold   tub holding me like the
sister I've missed

my sister   Ears   Texas   left after her passing   bloody hands
pointing to   her   dying   flood   an Act of God   holding
me like the sister I've missed

my sister   left after her passing   blood   her   tub
flooding   the sister I've missed

my sister   flood   I miss

my sister

Making Hay

Not the sound of the cutter,
but its vibrations—
my thighs numbing, tingling
as we crossed and recrossed
the stubbled field.
Not my job scanning for stones,
shouting in time for my husband
to stop, before the blades
could bend and break.
Not how fast it happened—
the cutter's teeth biting
a hidden granite shelf
sunk like a hungry mouth
into loam—not that,
but my tumbling
off the hot metal seat,
the sense of soaring
just before a fall.

After a Migraine

I hear mourning doves, robins and wrens,
quelling my brain's aural debris,
for days playing too loudly with itself.

I reflect how the mind in pain
became an echoing cave,
a world narrowed to a cell.

I longed to sip spring snow dripping from eaves,
watch long pine shadows lattice a snowy hill,
a world closed to me by that tightening.

Now, stepping into a clear day of sun,
of wind, of shadows on snow, of birdsong,
of streams loosening from ice,
I begin to understand where I've been.
With a heart newly opened, I take it all in.

Staying Alive

"It was just like this, but winter," she says to me,
gesturing to shadowed trees, as we rest on stones

above a chorus of summer thrush, as she starts to pale,
a bit tremulous, telling of snow-shoeing deep in hemlocks,

she and her husband of forty-eight years—how he crumpled
to his knees,
behind her in the snow, eyes staring,

"Unseeing," the coroner explained to her later,
"His optic nerve squeezed,
it only looked like he could."

How she cradled his head on her lap, as his heart seized,
pumped his chest with her mittened hands,

hummed, *Staying alive, Staying alive,* as 911 instructed,
until the Snowcat found them

a colder, darker hour later,
in the pathless woods,

and only then,
as they covered his eyes, did she wail.

My Uninvestigated Sister

Two weeks of overflow
flooding the neighbors
who never thought
to check on my sister.

"Suicide?"
Pete incises.

Jane tweezes:
"Then you'd turn off the taps."

Pete shrugs:
"Maybe not."
"But the blood?"

Jane guesses splinter
from the cop's hand
breaking down the door.

We'll never know.

This isn't Branagh's *Wallander,*
no caution tape,
no smart guy
fixing time of death—

only the homely cop
citing the date
he broke the door
though neighbors swear
the flood was older.

Not a crime,
just an overweight, middle-
aged woman
drowned in a tub—

a few drops of blood
in the sink.

My uninvestigated sister,
as alone
as she always insisted.

Dodes'ka-den, Dodes'ka-den

Watching Kurosawa's *Dodes'ka-den* at the theater,
in the early days dating my film professor,
his tweed beret cocked, his arm in the dark
pressing into mine, mine pressing back. Strolling
through Washington Square Park after rain,
vivid park lights shine in the ink-black night
like constellations. Like train tracks clacking,
I feel my life tugging *dodes'ka-den, dodes'ka-den,*
a steady rumble pulling me into my future,
or is it the sound of our unborn children, calling?

Poem to My Fallopian Tube

—after Lucille Clifton

I know
it wasn't
your fault
you almost killed me
you must have been scarred
by a little hook left
from an IUD
decades before

you let
so many pass through
a regular highway
of sperm and eggs
you did so well
year after year
two healthy babies
it was just that one egg
one day   snagged
started to grow

poor you bursting like
a regular Challenger disaster
in my abdomen's sky
exploding blood and tissue
what did it feel like for you I
felt like Christa McAuliffe's mother—

I can only hope
you were beyond hurt
when they scraped you out
when you became
medical waste

after that your twin
had to work twice as hard
against the odds
to channel one more healthy egg

dear left-sided pipe
of death
and life—
I remember you

Angels, Mermaids, and a Fox

Let your fingers do the walking,
wooed the old Yellow Pages ad.

In 2021 my fingers Yelp,
searching Houston crematoria.

Perpetual Peace has some good reviews,
Family First's okay,

but Sacred Choice seems best,
and the woman who answers my call

speaks in bell tones, calm and certain,
with motherly comfort,

her warm voice assuring,
"We will bring Claire to us."

In the meantime, my sister lies alone,
snow-cold on a metal slab

in the Medical Examiner's office.
As I speak with Lacey Fox, of Sacred Choice,

my granddaughter plasters angel stickers
across the polished wooden floor,

humming her mermaid song.
Tomorrow's work—scraping them off,

but today
I need these angels.

Ode on a Park Bench

My dog beside me, leaning gently in,
his furred warmth a solace

for mounting losses
I'm not contemplating

on this June morning,
this new-to-us city street,

his heat unneeded,
yet still, a comfort.

Amid the city's hurry
I find a different fullness, a quiet

so wide the sun seems to halt
in its cloudless sky,

brightening a dogwood tree
in white bloom, wafting

the sweetest scent of rose
I've ever known.

♀ ♀ ♀

She Who Loved Fine Cuisine

—for Pat Fargnoli, in memory

On the radio I hear a poem
After the Dream of My Death,
written by my dear friend.

She's recently died of cancer,
so it seems an eerie whispering
across The Great Abyss.

My knees weaken,
and for a few weightless moments
I tread water in liminal space.

My body sways, eyes fill,
but before I know it
vacation beckons me

back to the sun-dappled bay,
to my rumbling stomach,
to thoughts of lunch,

shrimp scampi, perhaps,
at *Pepe's On the Bay.*
And that's when I know—

Pat *is* speaking to me.

Special Delivery

As I walk our country road,
a FedEx van passes—
and it occurs to me
it might be her ashes,
from Texas—my sister,
finally coming to visit.

Clara's Gift

Stinging ocean wind bites with cold,
but I'm luscious in a new thick scarf

she crocheted—autumnal threads
of blue, orange, ocher,

chosen to match my russet coat.
Walking the windy coast,

she wraps me from neck to heart and further,
into places yarn alone cannot reach.

Watching the News From Afghanistan

Did I once travel in a rickety van to the north,
with my husband, two little children,

to the snowy peaks where Alexander crossed
toward Tibet?

Did it grow cold, did the electricity go out,
snow falling on the budding almond trees?

Did we hear men testing weapons in the market,
blasting Russian Kalashnikovs, American guns into the air?

Did I walk through crowds, head and shoulders covered
with my head bowed under a scarf?

Did we sit at cafés on unpaved streets,
sip sweet mint tea, among hungry, roving dogs?

Did my son trace circles in the dust,
as I nursed the baby, in the shadows of the Hindu Kush?

Do I hold my son's son
even closer, today,

as I watch videos of Afghan children
seeking refuge from mountains of guns,

dangling from landing gear,
falling from an escaping plane?

A Zoom Memorial

Sister Two of four wears sunglasses,
sits outside, insists she needs the sun's healing,
then complains she can't see
anyone else onscreen—surviving sisters,
cousins, grown children—
as Taos sun installs a wall between us

which, in this family,
counts as healing—blockade
our best way to safety—
as Sister Three embodied,
bunkered in her forty-year hermitage

and I, the youngest, Number Four,
find myself happy
in Zoom's communal boxes,
savoring the gentle familial faces,
each one a quiet offering

as Sister One, long medicated
for storms she never chose,
slouches in her lounge chair,
showing only the top of her head,
a few blowing wisps of hair—
hardly there at all.

The Good Kind of Chill

My butt gets cold as snow seeps in,
past the gloves I sit on.
The stream below opens in places
to show dark stones—

a portal to some memory of psychedelics,
or the time I got high on rapid breath,
breathing with intention—
a meditation taking me out of myself,

like Diane Seuss' poetry,
transporting me past whatever past I knew,
breaking me like Humpty Dumpty,
and I can't tell when I'll be my own again—

when words will mean what they once meant,
when wet was just cold or clammy,
splashed or submerged—

as when water on her hand
enacted the word to Helen.

Corduroys, warmer than jeans,
still let snow in—like a good book,
chilling from the butt up.

Diane blows my lid off too,
letting fresh air in,
as Emily would've wished.

I sit as snow melts and shifts,
opening a rabbit hole—
and I disappear, Alice-like, into it.

Mermaids

The agile octopus hunter passes
as we rest on slippery rocks,
his long-pronged fork just right
to find and net *presa viva*—live catch—
a true *cazador de pulpos*—
her Spanish lisping the z's,
rolling the r's in the way I love.

When I first heard that voice
I knew we'd go somewhere exotic
to New England—Honduras, Venezuela—
or, as it turns out, Galicia,
sitting on mossy stones,
three hundred miles
into our pilgrimage-without-belief,
to a holy Catholic site,
our wedding a year behind us.

She explains you never stab an octopus—
"for the ink matters—"
just as the black-clad sea god
brandishes his trident
and darts past,
letting us mermaids be.

No Headstone

Honoring my sister Claire
elicits some guesswork.

"I know," I say—to my kids, my wife,
grandkids, grandbaby—
"we'll place the ashes around the maple,
where the setting sun will touch."

A view of curving road, forest, layered hills
as far as the eye can see, and at our feet,
winter's slanting shadows and light.

So, no rock for her,
no words but the ones
we disperse into air,

the *thank you*, the wish
that she sees our family gathering,
hears the songs we offer.

Would that she could say
if it's enough.

My father's ashes
spread in New York Harbor,
my mother buried
in a cemetery near her house,

my half-sister
dissolved in a winding creek.

So many ways to sift
back into the planet,
so many returns

as we head home
in the forgetful snow.

Proof

I wonder what Chris—
or his consciousness—
is experiencing two days
past his death. Yesterday,
they carried his body from the house
as flutes played *Amazing Grace.*

Last week, we meditated—
his daughter on the bed beside him—
his body thin and shrunken,
green-striped pajamas, red blanket—
bright against his pallor.
As I did Reiki on his legs and feet,
he said he felt heat from my palms.

When I rose to leave,
we shook hands, bowed, said Namaste,
his face become a radiant smile.

Today, in the clean, spacious atria
of the car repair shop,
time opens. I help myself
to hot black tea, cookies,
and a book left on the chair—
a bit battered, as if dropped
from somewhere far above—
called *Proof of Heaven,*
and feel I need no other.

Whispering Death

Grief

is my sister

dying alone in her tub, the water overflowing

no one finding her

for two weeks

the policeman breaking down the door

the mystery of the blood

on the bathroom sink

her neighbor suing us

for the flood

rotting their
common wall

a package of ashes

arriving by FedEx truck

sprinkling them

beneath our sugar maple

our five-
year-old grandchild

whispering "death"

as snow falls on all of us

As Shadows Lengthen

As I go about my day,
coffee steaming in morning sun,

shadows of trees cast across snow,
I stand by a frozen stream,

beginning to melt—
widening portals of light through ice,

a bear invades a neighboring hive,
as Russia invades Ukraine,

rips its frames for larvae,
munching as I watch from the other side

of a broken stone wall,
as I remember how Stefan escaped

the Russian bear and Nazi predation,
stealing his parents, grandmother, sister—

his defecting to the West, where he later
married me. As Russia claws into Ukraine,

the bear coats its tongue with sweetness,
with no thought for the bees

made homeless in honey-less air—
as I go about my day,

walking with my wife on a country road,
her hand brushing mine,

as shadows lengthen,
two weeks short of spring.

Two Words

For my Dad—
who smuggled quinine to his men in prison camp.
His pre-war years on Yangtze riverboats,
studying Mandarin and tropical disease.

Who smuggled quinine to his men in prison camp,
while their captors died, enraging the commander.
Studying Mandarin and tropical disease,
he learned endurance.

While their captors died, enraging the commander,
water drops to the head, near starvation.
He learned endurance—
never betraying his quinine source.

Water drops to the head, near starvation,
a Chinese friend he would not name.
Never betraying his quinine source—
Doctor Foley kept the secret.

A Chinese friend he would not name,
through interrogation, the coma that followed.
Doctor Foley kept the secret—
there are two words for the kind of person he was.

Through interrogation, the coma that followed,
both beginning with H.
There are two words for the kind of person he was—
a healer first, a hero never to himself.

Both beginning with H—
who smuggled quinine to his men in prison camp.
A healer first, a hero never to himself.
He never betrayed his quinine source.

This Momentary Pasture

At home among late November woods,
a field between east and west light,
a cut of land thin as breath,

where we can see the setting sun,
so early, this near-winter afternoon
of blowing snow. We nestle like weeds

or fallen leaves on our gentle acres,
yet feel the unseen sea in the wind's rhythms,
in the moon rising from its wet trip

across oceans, in its watery shining
over our snowy yard, as we look into this night,
this moment—this elastic stretch of time—

as the glowing, unhurried planet curves beyond
the western hills that hide the sun,
the ever-turning-ness of our globe,

and looking in,
to know the forever of an instant,
pines shadowing snowy grass,

the pile of drying leaves,
those shining orbs of yellow light
that yesterday graced the poplar tree.

Into the Air

Sifting my estranged sister's papers
        after her death,

I find a 1996 Associate's Degree,
        Community College High Honors.

I see the sun flaring
        in my window's edge,

rosy light eking below hills,
        like my will to call her all those years.

All those years these woods
        kept hemming the valley,

all the fall days these trees
        kept shedding their leaves,

etching November in me.
        I find a recent photograph,

the only glimpse I've had for years,
        seeing in my sister's face

a mirror I never noticed,
        her smile a bit roguish.

"Warm congratulations on your degree"

I speak
        to empty air—

wonder if she hears.

Emergence

The bear from its lair.
Daffodils from their bulbs.
Grass from long-frozen roots,
streams from mountaintops,
filling woods with a ringing,
scent of cinnamon fern,
of rain-swollen puddles,
mirroring white birch,
then, a flutter of water,
a cardinal's wings,
and his pale mate's too.
A tentative woodpecker
on a hollow trunk.
Frogs and peepers silenced,
then not. Steps echoing
on pavement, squelching in mud,
the softness of mud cupping a sole,
each sound outside, a breath.

♀♀♀♀

Convergence

You are the convergence of two streams,
snow transformed to melt, to rush,

loosening of the earth,
soft soil exhaling breath, long held by ice.

You are the glints whitening
the waterfall's every wave,

the translucent pool,
white pebbles seen when the mind settles,

the breeze clattering last year's tenacious,
faded beech leaves, lifting sweet odors

of new grass, buds pressing through stems.
You are the green moss growing on a stone,

and a leaning maple tree's exposed roots,
washed by the rushing stream.

You are the brook and I am a rock,
bathed and softened by your touch.

Let's Go Out for Breakfast, I Say to Myself

I rush to the biggest Post Office at eight on Monday
so my card for the famous poet's birthday
won't arrive late, a forest of bamboo,
a panda dozing at ease—
which reminded me of him.

At the hipster café, my latte's bitter,
the bagel too salty to eat.
I spend the morning on a stool,
watching strangers on the street,
March winds buffeting eyes
with winter dust.

At lunch I meet my beloved,
her teaching gig done,
but the cool taco truck's closed,
not enough staff, explains the handmade sign.

We make our hungry way home,
and I stop at the railroad crossing,
where last November
her student backed onto the tracks,
didn't see the oncoming train.
I pause at the makeshift shrine—
a wooden cross, piles of basketballs,
plastic flowers, teddy bears.

Though the clerk said the card will arrive late,
though the coffee was undrinkable,
the bagel inedible,
the taco place closed,
though everyone has dust in their eyes,
for one moment I saw it—

a single ash leaf lifting upward,
spiraling over the railroad tracks,
brown, but catching light,
so it gleamed in passing,
spinning out of sight.

Little Darts

In the Winooski bank, a wispy-haired woman
in pink-flowered dress, matching pink purse,
forgets why she's there, explains her memory loss,
asks the teller to withdraw thirty dollars from savings,
then forgets how much she's asked for,
as the teller nods, smiles, reminds.
I've driven two hours to this branch,
to close my late sister's account.
I carry her dark blue checkbook,
handwriting neat and legible,
small numbers added, subtracted,
all I have left of her enclosed
in two Manila envelopes.
When she died, in her bathtub,
her new townhouse almost empty of furniture,
she must have known
she wouldn't be hosting anyone,
must have enjoyed the feeling
of owning so much private space.
At my turn in line, the bank manager
shakes my hand, looks into my eyes:
"I'm so very sorry for your loss."
I wonder if she sees my old grief,
for a sister lost to me
long before she passed,
snow-cold and distant as Pluto's farthest moon.

That night, I watch, from a lawn chair,
little darts of light
streaking and falling across a great darkness.

Ingonish Beach

At the far end
of a peninsula
narrowly tethered
to the mainland,
we stop
on a red-graveled road
to place a small pyramid
of stones at the Abbey,

offer a prayer
for Clara's ailing aunt Merce,
soak in the monk's view
of endless bay.

At Ingonish Beach
we receive a text
that Merce has passed.

We pause.

We plunge into the salty depths,
let the surf carry us,
cradled as we face such loss—
the same waves
bear Merce gently away.

Touching Stalin

My husband knew Stalin,
enough to eat a meal with him.

Stefan touching me was like
me touching Stalin.

Our grown children
still touch Stalin, touching me.

On a small screen, I watch Russians
touched by Putin
filling St. Petersburg Square,
against the invasion of Ukraine.

I see a Russian plane Putin sent
exploding, a parachutist
falling into the Black Sea.

Our grandchildren,
as yet untouched by Putin,
and free from school,
romp and sled in the field
where he and I once hayed,

where he lies buried,
but singing, through me,
beneath the thickening snow.

Tea and Sympathy

She drives all the way to my house,
up a steep hill in the woods of Vermont.

"I understand—this is someone's life,"
she offers, as she stamps and signs,
as I sign and sign, blue pen looping my name.

We sit at the kitchen table.
She pats our dog,
explaining how, in her free time,
she takes in elderly Labradors
at the end of their lives.

"Give them a year or two of happiness.
One just passed, last week.
I still wake at night to take him out."

We share spiced cookies,
Earl Grey tea,
as she tells me about her health,
a difficult teenage son,
how she loves to work on her own.

Meanwhile, I'm signing page after page—
tax documents, a deed—
as I sell my sister's townhouse in Texas,
the one she flooded
as she was dying in her tub.

Sheila places her cup in the sink,
scans the documents into her phone,
beams them off across the country.

As she leaves, I feel lighter,
freer of a sister I hadn't known well—
hadn't seen in forty years;

thankful for the sympathy—
a notary
whose stamp feels like kindness.

Communion

The chaplain's familiar words:
kingdom come, thy will be done,
stream over us,
my oldest sister barely awake,
hardly aware I've come
from hours away,
perched on a small folding chair,
squeezed between bed and IV pole,
in the stale-aired curtained room.
The chaplain moves her hand
above my sister's infected knee,
her whole body, then me;
takes a wafer from her tiny leather bag,
places it on my tongue, the first time
I've received the consecrated bread
since I was a barely-believing teen,
and I've forgotten: do I stow it
under my tongue, or let it melt on top?
I lift my sister's head gently up,
so she doesn't choke on the *Body of Christ,*
which, the chaplain and I agree,
Would be ironic.
We giggle like sisters, a playful communion
I've rarely known with my own.

Blackberries

I ask myself if summer
ever happened, if I haven't
eaten blackberries. And then—
I swear—an entire patch
where a bear once napped
beneath a maple sapling
jeweled with berries.
Today I stuff my face
with black, succulent juice,
purple lips, purple fingers—
a last taste to carry
through the ice
of what comes next.

The Mosquitoes of Tatamagouche

At a seaside campsite,
in afternoon heat,
swarms of mosquitoes
follow us inside the van.
We slam
screens down, still stuck
with dozens biting
necks, arms, ankles,
through thick socks
and the dog's fur,
till we kill them
one by one.
My wife, wearied
by difficult family news,
and driving strange highways,
sequestering with me
in the draining onslaught,
mutters something
she remembers
I said months ago,
and I bend my shoulder away—
stare out the window
as shadows lengthen
on the grassy field,
as the sting
of our angers
dissipates—
as we revise our plan,
rev the van,
and flee
the mosquitoes
of Tatamagouche.

Cloud Gazing

I walk the road daily to see if grazing cows
gaze at clouds the way Ritsos's did, in Greece.
I try to catch them at it, but usually
they just flex their muscled necks to measure me,
flick their ears. Yesterday, as early evening
swept the field with dusk shadows,
I spied three breaking trail through deep
new snow, lumbering toward a hemlock grove
where a black stream breaks through ice.
Among soft white hillocks they bent their heads,
slaked their thirst. One younger, nimbler,
galloped downhill to join them, leaping
and kicking up a powdery wake—
a cloud of snow all of us turned our eyes to see.

Yes

I see in close-up how intent Clara is,
measuring coffee for our morning.

She doesn't realize I am, for once,
not sailing to some uncharted island,
not lost in the news but here,
navigating deep waters
with my chosen shipmate.

Her lips moving a little starboard
of my port Yes—

a new settledness has landed
within sight of the horizon.

She doesn't know she's being seen.
She's being seen.

Neyaashiinigmiing Ringing

Neyaashiinigmiing, spoken like bells
ringing for the grace of the point's light
and cormorants diving—*Chippewa, Ojibwe*—
the Originals of splashing water.

Echoes of laughter have been the wind,
clear saltless seas on the lake,
and unceded First Nation Cape
playing on ancient limestone bluffs
crowns what was, and might have been.

Cold, deep water—
water lapping on the stone
gichigamiing water,
surface of the impossible—

the shadow of seagull-cry
against closed eyelids, thin and insistent,
pebbled shore, old growth pines.

How this world enters us in summer wind—
this *niibin noodinm*—
Croker *Neyaashiinigmiing*,
Point of Land Portage—

a point of oneness that might have been,
and yet may be, in *Nawash*,
in Harmony.

Cycles

Visiting the Bay of Fundy,
my favorite thing's the laundry
on a hot sunny day—
nothing else to do
but wait for the next cycle.

We count loonies, slip them into slots,
set clothes churning, then nap,
dreamless in the camper van,
harbored in the almost-empty lot.

After folding shirts and pants,
we walk across a mile of red mud
under pink sky—crabs scurrying,
shells and salty puddles still glistening—
covered just this morning

by deep tidal water, soon to be
drowned again, as waves tick off
the ages—minute by week by season—
as we sleep, and wake,
adding our little ripples to the sea.

Is This, Then, Poetry

If I tell you my dream—
shoulder blades crackling
with electricity as I fly,
diving into the earth
to carry up coffins—

do I resurrect
my father, my mother, my sister,
with words?

As you see them flicker
through my pen,
could I see them, too—

my long-gone parents
shoulder-to-shoulder, at ease,
and Claire, black-haired,
rising from water…

Claire

How my sister lived alone
in Texas, and died
alone in her bathtub,
how I received the call,
not having seen her
in forty years,

how her neighbors
described her as "odd,
with long gray hair"—
stuns me with an ache
I can't undo.

How she bequeathed me
a future I live in now—
a seaside house where I sit—
warms me,

looking into the dark night
at ghosts of snow
whipped up by the wind,
as the round moon lifts
in the black sky—
a December brightness I know is Claire,

clear as her name, this light,
this wide moon
shining down on all of us.

The Summer-Lessened Stream

I sit on a stone by a summer-lessened stream,
water low, boulders bare—
gentled by moss and springing ferns,

a shady reprieve from morning heat,
as I read again
the world is burning—

but not here, not yet,
where shade cools the pool enough
for a water strider to cast its shadow

on submerged banded schist,
skating in the dark space made
by my body leaning over it—

the forest as open to me
as to this little skimmer
to whom I whisper,

attending the variations—
strings, oboes, flute—
a thrush descending

through hemlock darkness,
where I forget for a moment
my eventual burning.

My dog and I
step off the path, linger
beside a stream that knows

the sun gleaming on mossed stone,
ferns swaying in a breeze
I don't yet feel.

Turning quietly
to stream and channel,
neither staying, nor going,

flowing.

Thanks

With much thanks to the Wednesday Poets—Brooke Herter-James, Jon Escher, Sarah Snyder, Jill Herrick-Lee, Lynne Byler, Deb Franzoni, Peg Brightman—and to the River Poets—Carol Westberg, Sue Burton, Anne Shivas, Clyde Watson—for ongoing poetry fellowship and good times: sharing new drafts, supporting one another.

Thank you to Ellen Bass, Marie Howe, Kim Addonizio, Rick Barot, Rosemerry Wahtola Trommer, for poetry inspiration and workshops.

Thank you to April Ossmann, for her untiring, keen editorial skills.

Thank you to Hayley Mitchell Haugen for believing in *Sister in a Different Movie* and bringing it to glorious life.

Thank you to Andrew Bonnycastle for letting us grace the cover with his vibrant painting, *The Three Graces.*

Thank you to attorney Riley Hetherington for his astute legal stewardship—leading me through the byways of administering my late sister's estate—and for his own deep appreciation of poetry.

To Kris Holt, who, while COVID kept us from leaving Vermont, helped us with all the nitty-gritty that needed doing around my sister's property in Houston.

To Lacey Fox of *A Sacred Choice*, who made all the arrangements to help us bring Claire's ashes home, where we could spread them beneath the maples in Vermont.

Thank you always to Clara, my wife, my steadfast first reader, my warmest comforter.

About the Author

Laura Foley is the author of eleven previous poetry collections including, most recently, *Sledding the Valley of the Shadow*, and *Ice Cream for Lunch*. She has won a Narrative Magazine Poetry Prize, Common Good Books Poetry Prize, Poetry Box Editor's Choice Chapbook Award, Bisexual Book Award, and others. Her work has been widely published in such journals as *Alaska Quarterly*, *Valparaiso Poetry Review*, *American Life in Poetry*, *One Art*, and anthologies such as *How to Love the World* and *Poetry of Presence*. She holds graduate degrees in Literature from Columbia University, and lives with her wife and their two romping canines on the steep banks of the Connecticut River in New Hampshire.

Sheila-Na-Gig Editions

www.ingramcontent.com/pod-product-compliance
Lightning Source LLC
Chambersburg PA
CBHW021339060726
47591CB00006B/2098